Release of Liability and Disclaimer

This book is intended solely for entertainment and educational purposes. The information contained herein reflects the opinions and experiences of the author and is not intended as financial, legal, or investment advice.

Readers should not interpret the content as a recommendation to buy, sell, or hold any asset, including Bitcoin, or to engage in any financial strategy. The concepts discussed are illustrative and may not be suitable for all individuals. Financial decisions involve significant risk, and past performance of any asset or strategy does not guarantee future results.

The author and publisher make no representations or warranties regarding the accuracy, completeness, or timeliness of the information provided. Readers are strongly encouraged to consult with qualified professionals, such as financial advisors, tax consultants, and legal experts, before making any decisions based on the information presented in this book.

By reading this book, you agree that the author and publisher shall not be held liable for any losses, damages, or other consequences arising directly or indirectly from your use of the information contained herein.

Copyright Statement

© **Rafael R. Rivera, 2024.**

All rights reserved. No part of this book may be reproduced, distributed, or transmitted in any form or by any means, including photocopying, recording, or other electronic or mechanical methods, without the prior written permission of the author or publisher, except in the case of brief quotations embodied in critical reviews and certain other noncommercial uses permitted by copyright law.

For permission requests, please contact author: rafarrivera@hotmail.com

Table of Contents

Release of Liability and Disclaimer.................................... 1
Copyright Statement.. 2
The Foundation of Modern Wealth...................................... 6
Bitcoin and the Dollar.. 9
    Complementing Traditional Finance................................. 9
        Why Bitcoin Makes the Dollar Better....................... 10
        A Personal Example: Sam's Story............................. 10
        How You Can Do the Same.. 11
        The Bigger Picture.. 12
Bitcoin as Your Liquidity Engine for Real Estate............ 14
        The Power of Leverage... 14
        Jane's Story: A Real-Life Example............................ 15
        Strategies for Real Estate Success........................... 16
        The Long Game: Passive Income Meets Growing Equity... 16
        A Friend's Perspective... 17
Bitcoin and Small Business Growth................................. 18
        What Makes Bitcoin a Perfect Fit for Small Businesses?... 18
        Mike's Story: How a Food Truck Business Doubled Revenue... 19
        Strategies for Small Business Owners..................... 20
        Avoid the Trap of Short-Term Selling........................ 21
        Visualizing the Bitcoin-Backed Business Model..... 21
        Building a Sustainable System................................... 22
        A Friend's Perspective... 22
Leveraging Bitcoin for the Stock Market......................... 24
        Why Combine Bitcoin and the Stock Market?......... 24
        A Practical Path: Emma's Story................................. 25
        Unlocking Advanced Stock Market Strategies....... 25
        Advanced Insights for Long-Term Success............ 27

    A Friend's Perspective.. 28
    Final Thoughts... 28
Bitcoin and Private Equity Opportunities................................ 30
    A Door to Exclusive Investments................................... 30
    David's Story: A Game-Changing Strategy.................. 31
    Why Private Equity Matters.. 31
    Building a Bitcoin-Driven Private Equity Strategy........ 32
    A Visual Roadmap.. 33
    Balancing Risk and Reward.. 34
    The Bigger Picture.. 34
    A Friend's Perspective.. 35
    Pro Tip... 35
    Final Thoughts... 35
Building a Flywheel – Bitcoin as the Wealth Engine............37
    The Flywheel Concept – A Personal Take.................. 37
    How Sam Built His Flywheel.. 38
    Breaking Down the Flywheel....................................... 38
    Why the Flywheel Works.. 40
    Pro Tips for Starting Your Flywheel..............................40
    A Visual Blueprint..41
    Advanced Insight: Balancing Risk................................ 42
    Why It's Worth It..42
    A Friend's Perspective.. 42
    Final Thoughts.. 43
Retirement with Bitcoin as Your Liquidity Core..................... 44
    A Fresh Take on Retirement Planning........................ 44
    Emma's Story: A Bitcoin-Powered Retirement........... 44
    Building Your Retirement Flywheel.............................. 45
    The Math Behind Bitcoin Retirement........................... 47
    A Flowchart for Bitcoin Retirement.............................. 47
    Why Bitcoin Works for Retirement............................... 48
    Pro Tips for a Bitcoin-Backed Retirement...................48
    A Friend's Perspective..49

    Advanced Insight: Long-Term Flexibility 50
    Final Thoughts 50
Bitcoin as the Pillar of Financial Independence 52
Advanced Bitcoin-Backed Investment Strategies 54
Building Generational Wealth with Bitcoin 55
    Preserving Wealth Across Generations 55
    Practical Steps for Preserving Wealth 56
    Bitcoin's Role in Estate Planning 57
    Asset Growth Over Decades 58
    Advanced Estate Planning Strategies 59
    Legacy Planning with Bitcoin 59
    Navigating Cross-Border Wealth Transfer 60
    Example: David's International Legacy 60
    The Role of Passive Income 61
    Advanced Insight: Bitcoin as a Family Business 62
    Final Thoughts 62
The Future of Bitcoin in a Decentralized Economy 64
    Bitcoin: An Evolution of Money 64
    Why Bitcoin Stands Apart from Other Cryptocurrencies. 65
    Bitcoin as a Timeless Trading Mechanism 66
    Bitcoin for Wealth Building 67
    Bitcoin for Generational Wealth Transfer 68
    Emerging Trends for Bitcoin in a Decentralized Economy 69
    Positioning Yourself for the Future with Bitcoin 70
    Example: Ethan's Strategy for the Decentralized Economy 71
    Why Bitcoin Is the Cornerstone of a Decentralized Future 71
    Final Thoughts 72

The Foundation of Modern Wealth

Bitcoin can function beyond just a simple digital currency. Bitcoin isn't just another form of money—it's a groundbreaking liquidity engine reshaping how individuals and institutions manage, preserve, and grow wealth. Acting as "digital gold," Bitcoin is a finite asset that offers long-term value storage and an increasing global acceptance in diverse markets.

Bitcoin works as a base liquid layer. Traditional financial systems are rife with inefficiencies, relying heavily on intermediaries, high transaction fees, and inflation-prone currencies. In contrast, Bitcoin eliminates many of these hurdles, offering a frictionless, borderless, and decentralized alternative. This makes it an ideal foundation for building modern wealth strategies.

- **Decentralization**: With no central authority, Bitcoin provides unparalleled financial autonomy.

- **Finite Supply:** Unlike fiat currencies, which can be printed at will, Bitcoin's supply is capped at 21 million coins, preserving its value over time.

- **Global Accessibility:** Bitcoin can be used anywhere, bypassing exchange rates and cross-border fees.

Think of Bitcoin as the ultimate base layer for your wealth strategy. Unlike fiat currencies that lose value due to inflation, Bitcoin offers a dual advantage: it appreciates over time while providing liquidity for other investments. By holding Bitcoin, you create a foundation that simultaneously stores value and serves as collateral for wealth-building ventures.

Example: Leveraging Bitcoin Without Selling It

Let's compare Bitcoin to dollars:

- **Scenario A – Dollars:** You keep your savings in a bank account earning minimal interest. Over time, inflation erodes your purchasing power, and your wealth shrinks.

- **Scenario B – Bitcoin:** Instead, you store your wealth in Bitcoin. When an investment opportunity arises—such as purchasing real estate or funding a business—you borrow against your Bitcoin holdings. This allows you to access capital without selling your Bitcoin, which continues to appreciate in value.

Case Study: Real Estate Investment

Jane has $100,000 worth of Bitcoin. She spots a real estate deal requiring $30,000 for a down payment.

Instead of selling her Bitcoin and losing exposure to its growth, she takes out a Bitcoin-backed loan. Over five years:

1. The property appreciates, yielding rental income and equity growth.

2. Her Bitcoin holdings increase in value, providing additional leverage for future investments.

This dual-growth strategy enables Jane to benefit from both the real estate market and Bitcoin's price appreciation.

The Ripple Effect on Wealth Building

Bitcoin as a liquidity engine extends beyond individual investments. It can power broader financial ecosystems, including:

1. **Small Business Growth:** Entrepreneurs can borrow against Bitcoin to fund operations, purchase inventory, or expand their businesses without diluting equity.
2. **Stock Market Investments:** Investors can access Bitcoin-backed loans to buy undervalued stocks during market dips, maximizing returns.

3. **Emergency Funds:** Bitcoin's liquidity ensures quick access to funds without incurring penalties or selling assets in adverse conditions.

Bitcoin and the Dollar

Complementing Traditional Finance

Let's talk about the relationship between Bitcoin and the dollar. A lot of people think they're at odds, like one has to win for the other to lose. But here's the thing—they're not enemies. In fact, when you use them together strategically, they complement each other beautifully.

Think about the dollar for a moment. It's a reliable workhorse, widely accepted and easy to use. Whether you're paying your bills, buying groceries, or booking a vacation, dollars are essential. But the dollar has one glaring flaw: it's constantly losing value because of inflation. Every year, the cost of living goes up, and what your dollars could buy last year doesn't stretch quite as far today.

Now let's bring Bitcoin into the picture. Bitcoin is like the secret sauce that can enhance your financial game. It's not tied to any government or central bank, and its supply is capped at 21 million coins, which means it can't be inflated away. Over time, Bitcoin has proven to grow in value, acting as a kind of "digital gold."

So, what's the magic formula? Combine the dollar's stability and liquidity with Bitcoin's ability to preserve and grow wealth. Together, they create a powerful, balanced financial system that puts you in control.

Why Bitcoin Makes the Dollar Better

Here's the thing about Bitcoin: it's an asset that you don't want to sell if you don't have to. Why? Because every time you sell, you're cutting yourself off from its future growth. But that doesn't mean it's locked away, out of reach. Instead of selling Bitcoin, you can use it as collateral to access dollar-denominated loans.

Think about that for a second. You're borrowing dollars, which you can spend freely, while your Bitcoin sits safely, continuing to grow in value. It's like using one tool to sharpen another.

But it doesn't stop there. Bitcoin also acts as a hedge against inflation. While your dollars may lose purchasing power over time, your Bitcoin holdings can grow, giving you a financial buffer that protects your wealth. This combination of liquidity and long-term value creation is a game-changer.

A Personal Example: Sam's Story

Let's bring this to life with a story. Meet Sam, a 40-something entrepreneur with an eye for opportunity. A few years ago, Sam started buying Bitcoin little by little. He didn't know much about it at first, but he figured it was worth a shot.

Fast forward to today, and Sam's Bitcoin stash is worth $100,000. One day, he notices a dip in the stock market. A few promising companies are trading at rock-bottom prices, and he knows this could be a chance to make some serious gains.

Here's what Sam does: instead of selling his Bitcoin, he uses it as collateral to borrow $50,000 in dollars. With that money, he buys shares in those undervalued companies. Over the next year, the stock market recovers, and his investments grow significantly.

Meanwhile, Bitcoin's value climbs too. By the end of the year, Sam has repaid his loan, reclaimed full ownership of his Bitcoin, and made a tidy profit on his stock investments.

The key takeaway? Sam didn't have to choose between Bitcoin and the dollar. He used them together, leveraging the strengths of each to create a win-win situation.

How You Can Do the Same

If you're wondering how to apply this to your own life, here's a step-by-step guide:

1. **Build Your Bitcoin Base:** Start by consistently investing in Bitcoin. Treat it like a long-term savings account.

2. **Stay Liquid:** Don't sell your Bitcoin when you need cash. Instead, explore platforms that allow you to borrow against your holdings.

3. **Look for Opportunities:** Use the borrowed dollars to invest in high-potential opportunities, like stocks, real estate, or even your own business.

4. **Repay and Reinvest:** As your investments grow, use the returns to repay your loan and secure your Bitcoin.

The Bigger Picture

At the end of the day, Bitcoin and the dollar aren't just financial tools—they're part of a broader strategy for building wealth and achieving financial freedom. The dollar gives you stability and access to everyday markets, while Bitcoin provides long-term growth and a hedge against inflation.

When you combine the two, you're not just keeping up with the times—you're staying ahead of them. This approach isn't about taking big risks; it's about making smart, calculated moves that set you up for success.

So, the next time someone asks you whether you're Team Bitcoin or Team Dollar, just smile and say, "Why not both?"

Bitcoin as Your Liquidity Engine for Real Estate

Let's have a real talk about real estate and Bitcoin. These two worlds might seem like they operate on different planes, but when you put them together, the possibilities are limitless. Real estate has always been one of the safest, most reliable ways to build wealth, and Bitcoin? Well, Bitcoin brings a new level of flexibility and scalability to the game.

Imagine this: you've got Bitcoin sitting in your digital wallet. It's growing in value over time, but right now, it's just sitting there, doing its thing. Meanwhile, you're eyeing a real estate market that's full of potential—properties that could generate rental income, fixer-uppers you could flip, or even land you could develop. What if I told you that your Bitcoin could be the key to unlocking these opportunities without selling a single Satoshi?

The Power of Leverage

Here's where it gets interesting. You don't have to sell your Bitcoin to get involved in real estate. Instead, you can leverage it. By using Bitcoin as collateral, you can take out loans in traditional currencies like dollars. This gives you immediate cash to invest in properties while keeping your Bitcoin intact and appreciating.

Think of Bitcoin as your financial engine. It powers your ability to invest without depleting your core wealth. The real beauty of this strategy? You're creating a cycle of growth. Your Bitcoin grows on one side, and your real estate investments generate income and equity on the other.

Jane's Story: A Real-Life Example

Let's talk about Jane. She's a young professional who started accumulating Bitcoin a few years ago. Over time, her Bitcoin holdings grew to be worth $300,000. Jane had always dreamed of getting into real estate, but she didn't want to sell her Bitcoin to fund it.

Instead, Jane took a different approach. She used her Bitcoin as collateral to secure a $100,000 loan. With that money, she bought a fixer-upper in a growing neighborhood. Over the next six months, she poured her energy into renovating the property—new flooring, updated kitchen, fresh paint. By the time she was done, the home's value had jumped significantly.
Jane sold the property for a $50,000 profit. She used that profit to repay her loan, and guess what? Her Bitcoin was still sitting there, untouched, and it had grown in value during that time. Now, she had both her

Bitcoin and a nice chunk of cash to reinvest in her next deal.

Strategies for Real Estate Success

The cool thing about combining Bitcoin and real estate is how many doors it opens. Here are a few strategies to consider:

1. **Securing Down Payments:** Use Bitcoin-backed loans to fund down payments on rental properties. This gives you access to the real estate market without selling your Bitcoin.
2. **Flipping Homes:** Borrow against your Bitcoin to purchase and renovate properties, then sell them for a profit. It's a great way to multiply your investment.
3. **Building a Portfolio:** Use Bitcoin as revolving capital to gradually acquire a diversified real estate portfolio. As your properties generate income, you can reinvest it into more opportunities.

The Long Game: Passive Income Meets Growing Equity

Let's not forget about the long-term benefits of combining Bitcoin with real estate. Rental properties, for example, can generate steady passive income. When you pair that with Bitcoin's potential for long-term appreciation, you're setting yourself up for a dual-stream of wealth creation.

Think about it like this: your rental property provides monthly cash flow, while your Bitcoin acts as an appreciating asset that you can leverage again and again. Over time, this creates a powerful financial ecosystem that works for you, not the other way around.

A Friend's Perspective

Here's the thing, and I'm saying this as a friend: real estate and Bitcoin are both amazing tools, but they're even better when you use them together. The trick is to think strategically and stay patient. Don't rush to sell your Bitcoin or overextend yourself with too many loans. Instead, focus on building a balanced approach that lets both your Bitcoin and your real estate investments thrive.

I know it can feel overwhelming at first. The idea of leveraging one asset to build another might seem risky, but when you take the time to understand how it works, it's incredibly empowering. You're not just building wealth—you're creating a system that keeps growing and evolving with you.

So, the next time you look at your Bitcoin wallet, don't just see it as digital money. See it as the engine that can drive you into the real estate market and beyond. With the right mindset and strategy, you've got everything you need to make it happen.

The possibilities are endless, and you've got the tools to start. Let's get to work!

Bitcoin and Small Business Growth

Hey there, let's talk about a game-changing way to grow your small business. We're talking about Bitcoin—not just as an investment but as a tool to take your business to the next level. Think of Bitcoin as your secret weapon—a liquidity bridge that helps you scale your operations, expand your reach, or even weather tough times without jumping through the hoops of traditional financing.

If you're a small business owner, you know how challenging it can be to get access to cash when you need it most. Loans come with high interest rates and paperwork, while using your savings can leave you vulnerable. Bitcoin offers a different path—a way to borrow without losing ownership of your assets. Let's break it down.

What Makes Bitcoin a Perfect Fit for Small Businesses?

Bitcoin isn't just "digital money." It's an asset you can leverage without selling. This means you can use its value to grow your business while keeping your Bitcoin intact and appreciating over time. Think of it as equity—like owning a piece of your business that you can borrow against, over and over.

Here's a simple flow of how it works:

1. **Hold Bitcoin:** Accumulate Bitcoin as part of your financial strategy.

2. **Borrow Against It:** Use Bitcoin as collateral to secure loans in traditional currency.

3. **Invest in Growth:** Use the loan to fund business operations, expansion, or inventory.

4. **Repay the Loan:** With profits generated from your investment, repay the loan while your Bitcoin remains intact.

5. **Repeat:** As Bitcoin appreciates, its borrowing power grows, letting you fund future opportunities.

Mike's Story: How a Food Truck Business Doubled Revenue

Let's look at Mike, a small business owner who runs a food truck. His business is thriving, and he's ready to expand, but traditional loans are out of reach. He's already stretched with inventory costs, and the last thing he wants is another high-interest loan.

Instead, Mike takes a different route. He's been holding Bitcoin for a few years, and its value has grown significantly. He uses some of his Bitcoin as collateral to secure a $50,000 loan. With that money, he buys a second food truck and hires a small team.

In just a few months, his revenue doubles. The new truck pays for itself in no time, and Mike uses the additional profits to repay the loan. Meanwhile, his Bitcoin remains untouched, growing in value as a long-term asset.
Now, Mike has not just one but two revenue-generating trucks and an appreciating asset in Bitcoin. That's the power of leveraging Bitcoin for business growth.

Strategies for Small Business Owners

Here are some practical ways you can use Bitcoin to grow your business:

1. **Scaling Inventory:** During peak seasons, use Bitcoin-backed loans to stock up on inventory without depleting your cash reserves. This ensures you're ready to meet demand without compromising your financial stability.

2. **Expanding Locations:** Thinking about opening a new store or buying new equipment? Borrow against Bitcoin to fund expansion plans while keeping your capital for day-to-day operations.

3. **Franchising:** If your business is franchise-ready, Bitcoin can provide the liquidity you need to launch multiple locations.

4. **Emergency Liquidity:** When cash flow is tight, Bitcoin can act as a safety net, helping you cover unexpected expenses without resorting to high-interest loans.

Avoid the Trap of Short-Term Selling

Here's a pro tip: Avoid the temptation to sell your Bitcoin for quick cash. Selling may solve immediate problems, but it comes at the cost of long-term growth. Instead, focus on building systems where your business profits cover loan repayments. This way, you preserve your Bitcoin's value and set yourself up for future opportunities.

Visualizing the Bitcoin-Backed Business Model

Bitcoin-Backed Business Model

1. Accumulate Bitcoin
   ↓
2. Use as Collateral
   ↓
3. Borrow Cash
   ↓
4. Invest in Growth
   ↓
5. Repay Loan with Profits
   ↓
6. Retain Growing Asset

Building a Sustainable System

The beauty of using Bitcoin in your business is that it's not a one-time play—it's a system you can use over and over. As your business grows and your Bitcoin appreciates, you create a feedback loop of opportunity. Each time you borrow against your Bitcoin, you're tapping into its growing value to fund your business goals without ever depleting your reserves.

A Friend's Perspective

As someone who's been where you are, let me tell you—this isn't just a cool idea; it's a mindset shift. Bitcoin lets you think bigger. It's about playing the long game while solving immediate challenges.

So, whether you're running a food truck, a boutique, or a tech startup, start thinking about Bitcoin as more than an investment. It's your ticket to sustainable growth, giving you the flexibility to take risks, scale your business, and build a solid foundation for the future. Let's make it happen!

Leveraging Bitcoin for the Stock Market

Let's chat about one of the most exciting opportunities Bitcoin offers: the ability to leverage its liquidity to dive into the stock market. Imagine having a financial engine that doesn't just sit there but actively powers your investments. That's what Bitcoin does—it's not just a savings account; it's a gateway to unlocking bigger possibilities without selling your core asset.

Why Combine Bitcoin and the Stock Market?

Bitcoin is revolutionary as a long-term, appreciating asset. The stock market, on the other hand, offers opportunities for growth, dividends, and passive income. When you combine the two, you're creating a dynamic strategy where Bitcoin becomes the foundation, funding your forays into equities while continuing to grow in value.

Here's the magic: instead of selling your Bitcoin to invest in stocks, you borrow against it. This lets you maintain your Bitcoin holdings, benefit from its appreciation, and use the borrowed funds to make strategic stock market investments. You're essentially putting your money to work in two places at once.

A Practical Path: Emma's Story

Meet Emma. She's held Bitcoin for years, watching its value soar. But rather than just sitting on her Bitcoin, she decides to make it work harder. She uses a portion of her Bitcoin as collateral to take out a $20,000 loan. With this liquidity, Emma invests in a mix of growth stocks and dividend-paying ETFs. Her strategy is simple:

- Growth stocks for capital appreciation.
- Dividend ETFs for steady income.

Over time, the dividends from her ETFs not only cover the interest on her loan but also provide extra income. Meanwhile, the stocks she picked for growth see significant gains.

The best part? Emma's Bitcoin remains untouched and continues to grow in value. At the end of ten years, she's built a diversified portfolio generating passive income, all while her Bitcoin is worth far more than when she started.

Unlocking Advanced Stock Market Strategies

Using Bitcoin as your liquidity engine gives you access to strategies that can amplify your returns. Here are some ideas to consider:

1. **Dividend Reinvestment:** Invest in dividend-paying stocks or ETFs. Use the dividends to cover your loan interest and reinvest the rest into Bitcoin during market dips.

2. **Covered-Call Strategies:** Own stocks and sell call options to generate passive income. Use these premiums to buy more Bitcoin or diversify into other assets.

3. **Index Funds for Stability:** If you're looking for lower risk, consider using your borrowed funds to invest in index funds like the S&P 500. Over time, these funds offer steady growth and dividends.

Visualizing the Strategy

Here's how it all works in a simple flow:

Leveraging Bitcoin for the Stock Market

1. Accumulate Bitcoin
   ↓
2. Use Bitcoin as Collateral
   ↓
3. Borrow Liquidity
   ↓
4. Invest in Stocks/ETFs
   ↓
5. Earn Returns (Growth, Dividends, Income)
   ↓
6. Reinvest Gains Back into Bitcoin or Stocks

This cycle creates a feedback loop of wealth-building, where each asset complements the other.

Advanced Insights for Long-Term Success

1. **Timing the Market:** Use stock market gains to buy more Bitcoin during bearish cycles. This compounding approach builds wealth in both assets.

2. **Mitigating Risk:** Diversify your stock portfolio with a mix of growth and income-generating assets. This ensures stability while taking advantage of Bitcoin's volatility for higher returns.

3. **Stay Liquid:** Maintain a buffer of accessible funds to cover unexpected expenses or loan repayments.

A Friend's Perspective

Let me level with you: this isn't about gambling or taking unnecessary risks. It's about being smart with your money. By leveraging Bitcoin's liquidity, you're opening doors to opportunities that might otherwise feel out of reach. You're not just building wealth—you're creating a system where your assets work together to generate consistent growth.

Imagine a future where your investments are diversified, your Bitcoin is untouched and growing, and your stock market portfolio is paying you dividends. That's the kind of financial freedom this strategy can create.

Final Thoughts

The combination of Bitcoin and the stock market isn't just a strategy; it's a mindset. It's about thinking bigger and smarter, using the tools available to you to create a sustainable, scalable financial future.

So, what's stopping you? Whether you're a seasoned investor or just starting, leveraging Bitcoin for the stock market could be the move that sets you up for long-term success. Dive in, experiment, and make it your own. Let's build something amazing together!

Bitcoin and Private Equity Opportunities

Imagine being able to invest in high-potential startups, cutting-edge technologies, or even your dream business venture, without draining your bank account or liquidating your assets. With Bitcoin as your financial anchor, these opportunities become not just possible but accessible. Private equity investments—traditionally reserved for well-capitalized investors—are now within reach when you use Bitcoin-backed liquidity wisely.

Let's dive into how Bitcoin empowers you to tap into this lucrative world, build wealth, and retain your long-term asset at the same time.

A Door to Exclusive Investments

Private equity is like the VIP section of investing. These are the deals where major wealth is created: startups, venture capital funds, and niche projects in industries like AI, biotech, and renewable energy. Traditionally, accessing these opportunities required a significant amount of upfront capital. But with Bitcoin, you have a way in.

By borrowing against your Bitcoin, you can fund private equity ventures while keeping your Bitcoin intact. This strategy lets you maintain your base of wealth while benefiting from the explosive growth potential of private equity investments.

David's Story: A Game-Changing Strategy

Let me tell you about David. He's held Bitcoin for years, watching its value climb steadily. But rather than sitting back and waiting for the price to rise, David decided to take a calculated risk.

David borrows $50,000 against his Bitcoin and invests in a promising biotech startup through a private equity fund. Over the next five years, the startup develops groundbreaking technology, and its valuation skyrockets. David's initial stake grows to $500,000.

What does David do? He repays the loan using a portion of his profits, reinvests another chunk into Bitcoin, and diversifies the rest across other private equity deals. By leveraging his Bitcoin, David turned an opportunity into a massive win, all while keeping his Bitcoin holdings intact and appreciating.

Why Private Equity Matters

Private equity investments offer several unique advantages:

1. **High Growth Potential:** Startups and niche companies often have the capacity for exponential growth, offering returns that traditional stocks and bonds can't match.

2. **Portfolio Diversification:** Adding private equity to your investment mix reduces reliance on volatile markets like stocks or real estate.

3. **Influence and Involvement:** Private equity often allows you to play an active role in the companies you invest in, aligning your investments with your values or expertise.

Building a Bitcoin-Driven Private Equity Strategy

If David's story inspired you, here's how you can follow a similar path:

1. **Borrow Smartly:** Use Bitcoin-backed loans to fund your private equity investments. Be mindful of loan terms, interest rates, and repayment schedules.
2. **Research and Due Diligence:** Investigate potential investments thoroughly. Look at the

company's management, business model, market potential, and financial health.

3. **Diversify Across Sectors:** Don't put all your eggs in one basket. Spread your investments across high-growth sectors like AI, fintech, renewable energy, and health tech.

4. **Plan for the Long Term:** Private equity investments typically take years to mature. Be patient and let the businesses grow.

A Visual Roadmap

Here's a simple flow to show how Bitcoin can power your private equity ventures:

Bitcoin-Driven Private Equity Strategy

1. Accumulate Bitcoin
↓
2. Use Bitcoin as Collateral
↓
3. Borrow Liquidity
↓
4. Invest in Private Equity
↓

5. Monitor & Support Investment Growth
   ↓
6. Realize Profits and Reinvest

This loop allows you to maximize returns while keeping your Bitcoin growing in the background.

Balancing Risk and Reward

Private equity investments are not without risk. Some ventures might fail, while others could exceed expectations. To manage this, balance your portfolio with a mix of:

1. **High-Risk, High-Reward Projects:** Startups with massive potential but uncertain outcomes.

2. **Stable, Lower-Risk Investments:** Established private companies or funds with consistent returns.

By diversifying, you mitigate losses and amplify gains, ensuring your overall portfolio remains resilient.

The Bigger Picture

Bitcoin is more than just a store of value; it's your partner in creating new opportunities. With its backing, you can participate in groundbreaking innovations, support ideas you believe in, and grow your wealth at a scale that traditional savings simply can't match.

A Friend's Perspective

Think of Bitcoin as your golden ticket to exclusive rooms that were previously closed off to all but the wealthiest investors. It gives you leverage—not just financial, but strategic. You can make moves that align with your goals and values, all while holding onto an appreciating asset.
When you're at a point in life where you want to do more than just "play it safe," this strategy allows you to dream bigger. You're not just investing in companies—you're investing in the future, and Bitcoin is the vehicle that gets you there.

Pro Tip

When your equity stakes pay off, don't just cash out. Reinvest some of the profits back into Bitcoin during dips. This creates a compounding effect, growing your wealth across two dynamic, high-reward assets.

Final Thoughts

Private equity investing isn't just for the elite anymore. With Bitcoin as your liquidity engine, you're already part of the next generation of savvy investors. Whether it's funding the next big thing in AI or supporting a sustainable energy project, Bitcoin-backed private equity investments can position you as a forward-thinking investor.

The opportunities are endless. All it takes is the willingness to think outside the box and let Bitcoin be the bridge to something extraordinary.

Building a Flywheel – Bitcoin as the Wealth Engine

What if I told you that building wealth could be as simple as creating a system where your investments continually feed into one another, growing stronger and more sustainable with time? That's what the flywheel approach is all about.

Bitcoin isn't just a tool for storing value or making quick gains—it can be the engine that powers your entire financial strategy. By leveraging its unique characteristics and combining them with diversified investments, you create a cycle of compounding growth that minimizes risk while maximizing rewards.

The Flywheel Concept – A Personal Take

Think of a flywheel. At first, it takes effort to get it moving. You have to push and push, but once it gains momentum, it spins effortlessly, powered by its own weight and energy.

In wealth building, Bitcoin is the weight and the engine. It acts as your starting point, allowing you to borrow against its value and fund other investments—whether it's real estate, stocks, or private equity. The returns from those investments then flow back into Bitcoin, increasing its value and enabling you to borrow even more. It's a self-sustaining cycle that grows stronger with every turn.

How Sam Built His Flywheel

Let's talk about Sam, a regular guy with big financial goals. He starts with $100,000 in Bitcoin. Instead of letting it sit idle, he borrows $30,000 against it and uses the money to purchase a rental property.
The property generates rental income that not only covers his loan repayments but also provides extra cash flow. Meanwhile, his Bitcoin appreciates.

A year later, Sam uses his now $120,000 in Bitcoin as collateral for another $30,000 loan. This time, he invests in dividend-paying stocks. The dividends give him a steady income, which he reinvests into Bitcoin during price dips. Over the years, this cycle builds a diversified portfolio of appreciating assets and income streams—all starting with Bitcoin.

Breaking Down the Flywheel

Here's how the flywheel works in practice:

1. **Bitcoin as Collateral**

- Borrow against Bitcoin's appreciating value instead of selling it.
- Keep your Bitcoin intact to benefit from long-term growth.

2. Strategic Investments

- Use Bitcoin-backed loans to fund income-generating assets like real estate or dividend stocks.
- Diversify with higher-risk, higher-reward opportunities like private equity or growth stocks.

3. Income and Returns

- Use rental income, stock dividends, or investment profits to repay loans.
- Allocate surplus returns into new investments or back into Bitcoin.

4. Compounding Growth

- As Bitcoin appreciates, your borrowing capacity increases.
- Reinvest profits to fuel the next round of investments, creating a cycle of compounding growth.

Why the Flywheel Works

The genius of the flywheel approach lies in its balance of risk and reward. By combining Bitcoin's growth potential with income-generating assets like real estate or dividend stocks, you create a diversified portfolio that's resilient in different economic climates.

When markets are booming, your growth-focused investments—Bitcoin and stocks—generate significant returns. During downturns, income from real estate or dividends provides stability, allowing you to weather the storm without selling your assets.

Pro Tips for Starting Your Flywheel

1. **Start Small**
   Begin with manageable investments. Borrow conservatively and focus on stable assets to get your flywheel moving.

2. **Diversify Smartly**
   Balance growth-focused investments with income-generating ones.

For example:

- Real estate for steady cash flow.
- Bitcoin for long-term appreciation.
- Dividend stocks for passive income.

3. **Reinvest Strategically**
Use market dips to reinvest profits into Bitcoin or other undervalued assets.

4. **Monitor and Adjust**
Keep an eye on your portfolio and rebalance as needed. For instance, if Bitcoin's value spikes, consider leveraging it further to fund additional investments.

A Visual Blueprint

Here's a simplified flowchart of the flywheel strategy:

Bitcoin → Borrow → Invest in Real Estate/Stocks → Generate Income → Repay Loan → Reinvest Profits → Back to Bitcoin

Every cycle strengthens the next, creating a self-sustaining loop that builds wealth over time.

Advanced Insight: Balancing Risk

While the flywheel is powerful, it's essential to approach it with care. Over-leveraging can expose you to unnecessary risk, especially if Bitcoin's value fluctuates. Always maintain a safety buffer—only borrow a fraction of your Bitcoin's value to protect yourself during market corrections.

Why It's Worth It

The flywheel approach isn't just about building wealth; it's about creating a system that works for you. It allows you to leverage opportunities without sacrificing long-term growth. Instead of selling assets to fund your next move, you use them as a foundation for future success.

A Friend's Perspective

Think of the flywheel as your financial fitness plan. At first, it might feel like a lot of effort—balancing loans, investments, and repayments. But as you get into the rhythm, it becomes second nature. You'll start to see results: your Bitcoin grows, your real estate portfolio expands, and your stocks generate passive income.

Soon, you'll realize that you're not just working for money—your money is working for you.

Final Thoughts

The flywheel is the ultimate strategy for anyone looking to maximize Bitcoin's potential. By combining it with a diversified investment approach, you create a system that grows wealth consistently and sustainably.
It's not just about making money; it's about building a financial future that's resilient, dynamic, and uniquely yours. Whether you're starting with $10,000 or $1 million, the principles remain the same: start small, think long-term, and let the flywheel do the heavy lifting.

Your financial journey doesn't have to be complicated—it just needs the right engine. And for the modern investor, Bitcoin is the perfect one to get you there.

Retirement with Bitcoin as Your Liquidity Core

Retirement planning can feel overwhelming. How do you ensure you'll have enough income to sustain your lifestyle without running out of money? This is where Bitcoin can become your secret weapon—a foundational liquidity layer that lets you live comfortably while your wealth continues to grow.

Think of it as creating a retirement plan that not only supports you now but also keeps building wealth for the future. The beauty of Bitcoin lies in its dual function as an appreciating asset and a liquidity engine, which allows you to access funds without selling off your core holdings.

A Fresh Take on Retirement Planning

Retirement used to be all about stockpiling assets and slowly drawing them down over time. While this approach works, it can feel restrictive. Imagine a retirement strategy that lets you keep your principal investments intact while generating passive income. Bitcoin makes this possible by giving you the ability to borrow against its value.

Emma's Story: A Bitcoin-Powered Retirement

Let's talk about Emma. She's in her early 50s and looking to secure her retirement. Emma owns $500,000 worth of Bitcoin and wants to create a diversified income stream. Instead of selling her Bitcoin, she takes out a $100,000 loan against it.

She uses this loan to invest in a mix of high-dividend ETFs and a small rental property. Over the next 20 years:

- The ETFs generate consistent dividend income, which she reinvests into more shares.

- The rental property provides steady cash flow, which she uses to pay off the Bitcoin loan.

By the time Emma retires, she has a growing Bitcoin base, a portfolio of dividend-paying stocks, and a fully paid-off rental property. Her financial future is secure, and she's built a system that supports her lifestyle without depleting her assets.

Building Your Retirement Flywheel

Here's how you can create a similar strategy:

1. **Start with Bitcoin as Collateral**

    - Borrow conservatively—aim for loans that are 25-30% of your Bitcoin's value to minimize risk.
    - Keep your Bitcoin intact to benefit from long-term appreciation.

2. **Diversify Retirement Investments**

    - Focus on assets that generate cash flow, like dividend-paying ETFs, rental properties, or private annuities.
    - Avoid risky, high-volatility investments during retirement years. Stability is key.

3. **Reinvest Surplus Income**

    - Use surplus income from your investments to reinvest in Bitcoin during market dips or to fund additional retirement assets.

4. **Build a Sustainable System**

    - Structure your investments so that the returns outpace the loan interest. This creates a self-sustaining system where you're never "spending down" your principal assets.

The Math Behind Bitcoin Retirement

Let's break it down with numbers. Assume you own $300,000 worth of Bitcoin:

- You take a $75,000 loan at a 6% annual interest rate.
- You invest $50,000 in high-dividend ETFs yielding 4% annually and $25,000 in a small rental property.

Yearly returns:

- ETFs: $2,000 (dividends)
- Rental property: $3,000 (net income)

Total: $5,000

Your loan interest costs $4,500 annually, leaving you with a $500 surplus. As your ETF shares and Bitcoin grow in value, this surplus increases, giving you more flexibility.

A Flowchart for Bitcoin Retirement

Here's how the system flows:

Bitcoin → Borrow → Invest in Cash Flow Assets → Generate Passive Income → Repay Loan → Reinvest Surplus → Back to Bitcoin

This loop creates a retirement system where your wealth grows alongside your income streams, providing both security and flexibility.

Why Bitcoin Works for Retirement

Bitcoin is a unique retirement tool because it's both liquid and appreciating. Traditional retirement assets, like 401(k)s and pensions, are excellent for stability but lack the dynamic growth potential that Bitcoin offers. By combining the two, you get the best of both worlds:

- Stability through diversified investments.
- Growth through Bitcoin's long-term appreciation.

Pro Tips for a Bitcoin-Backed Retirement

1. **Borrow Wisely**

   - Stick to low loan-to-value (LTV) ratios, ideally under 30%. This ensures you won't face margin calls during market downturns.

2. **Focus on Cash Flow**

   - Prioritize investments that generate steady, reliable income.
   - Think rental properties, dividend ETFs, or private annuities.

3. **Plan for Volatility**

   - Bitcoin's price can swing dramatically. Keep a buffer of liquid assets to cover unexpected expenses without needing to sell Bitcoin.

4. **Use Surpluses Strategically**

   - Reinvest surplus income into Bitcoin during dips or into additional retirement investments. This compounds your wealth over time.

A Friend's Perspective

Here's the thing: retirement doesn't have to mean giving up on growth. I know it sounds counterintuitive, but with Bitcoin as your foundation, you can create a plan that balances income and appreciation.

Imagine being able to enjoy your retirement without constantly worrying about running out of money. You'd have passive income streams supporting your daily life and a growing Bitcoin reserve securing your long-term future. It's like having your cake and eating it too.

Advanced Insight: Long-Term Flexibility

One of the best things about using Bitcoin for retirement is the flexibility it provides. Unlike traditional retirement accounts, which often have penalties for early withdrawals, Bitcoin-backed loans allow you to access liquidity whenever you need it.

Need funds for an unexpected medical expense? Borrow against your Bitcoin. Want to help your grandkids with college? Borrow a little more. The key is to keep your borrowing conservative and focus on sustainable income streams.

Final Thoughts

Retirement planning with Bitcoin isn't just about preparing for the future—it's about building a life where you can thrive, not just survive. By leveraging Bitcoin's unique strengths, you create a system that supports you now and continues to grow over time.

It's not about taking unnecessary risks; it's about using smart strategies to maximize what you already have. With the right approach, Bitcoin can be the cornerstone of a retirement plan that's flexible, sustainable, and full of possibilities.

So, as you think about your retirement goals, ask yourself: How can Bitcoin help me create a future that's both secure and dynamic? With a little planning and a lot of patience, the answer might surprise you.

Bitcoin as the Pillar of Financial Independence

Bitcoin isn't just an asset; it's a tool for achieving financial independence through strategic liquidity. By using Bitcoin as a base, you gain access to opportunities that traditional savings or retirement accounts cannot offer.

Building Independence with Bitcoin:

- **Passive Income Engine:** Borrow against Bitcoin to invest in income-generating assets, such as rental properties or dividend-paying stocks.
- **Risk Buffer:** Bitcoin's long-term appreciation can offset risks from short-term investments or economic downturns.
- **Portfolio Diversification:** Bitcoin acts as a hedge against inflation and market volatility, complementing other investments.

Example in Action:

Sophia starts with $50,000 in Bitcoin. She borrows $15,000 to invest in a rental property and uses rental income to repay the loan. Over ten years, the property value and Bitcoin both grow, creating a dual source of wealth.

Advanced Insight:

By treating Bitcoin as a financial springboard, you build

multiple revenue streams while keeping your core asset growing in value.

Advanced Bitcoin-Backed Investment Strategies

This chapter delves into complex strategies that allow you to leverage Bitcoin for high-yield opportunities while minimizing risk.

Key Strategies:

1. **Dollar-Cost Averaging into Bitcoin-Backed Investments:**
   Use small, recurring loans against Bitcoin to systematically invest in diversified assets. This reduces the risk of overleveraging while compounding returns over time.

2. **Compound Reinvestment:**

   - Use returns from investments (e.g., rental income, dividends) to buy more Bitcoin.
   - As Bitcoin's value grows, your borrowing capacity increases, creating a compounding effect.

3. **Leveraged Growth during Market Cycles:**
   Borrow during bear markets when Bitcoin is undervalued and invest in high-growth opportunities. Repay loans during bull markets, locking in gains.

Example: Mark borrows $10,000 against his Bitcoin to invest in renewable energy stocks. As the market grows, he sells a portion of his stocks to repay the loan and reinvests profits into Bitcoin during a price dip.

Pro Tip:

Maintain a safe loan-to-value (LTV) ratio to avoid liquidation during market volatility. A diversified portfolio reduces risk while amplifying returns.

Building Generational Wealth with Bitcoin

Bitcoin isn't just a tool for wealth accumulation; it's a vehicle for building and preserving generational wealth. In a world where traditional assets are often eroded by inflation, economic instability, or excessive taxation, Bitcoin offers a unique alternative. Its decentralized, borderless, and deflationary nature makes it a powerful asset for securing your family's financial future across generations.

Preserving Wealth Across Generations

For centuries, families have sought to protect their wealth against the ravages of time and economic uncertainty. Traditionally, this has involved holding assets like real estate, gold, or stocks. While these remain valuable, they are not without risks. Real estate

markets can crash, currencies can devalue, and stocks are subject to corporate risks.
Bitcoin, on the other hand, provides a hedge against many of these challenges:

- **Decentralization:** No single entity can control Bitcoin, shielding it from geopolitical risks and government overreach.

- **Deflationary Nature:** With a capped supply of 21 million coins, Bitcoin's scarcity ensures its value isn't diluted over time like fiat currencies.

- **Borderless Transfers:** Families with members across different countries can seamlessly transfer Bitcoin without bureaucratic red tape.

Practical Steps for Preserving Wealth

1. **Long-Term Holding Strategies**
   Treat Bitcoin as your family's "digital gold." By holding it securely over decades, you protect wealth against inflation and economic downturns.

2. **Diversify Around Bitcoin**
   Pair Bitcoin with other assets, like real estate or dividend stocks, to create a balanced wealth preservation strategy. Use Bitcoin's long-term

appreciation potential as the growth engine of your portfolio.

3. **Educating Future Generations**
   Knowledge transfer is as important as wealth transfer. Equip your heirs with the financial literacy and technical skills to manage Bitcoin effectively.

Bitcoin's Role in Estate Planning

Estate planning with Bitcoin requires a forward-thinking approach. While it shares similarities with traditional assets, Bitcoin's unique characteristics demand tailored solutions.

1. **Creating a Bitcoin Trust**
   Setting up a trust that holds Bitcoin ensures its secure transfer to future generations. Trusts can also generate income by leveraging Bitcoin for loans or staking.

2. **Digital Inheritance Frameworks**
   Develop a clear plan for accessing and managing your Bitcoin, including:
   - Wallet access keys.
   - Instructions for using wallets or exchanges.

- A contingency plan for heirs unfamiliar with cryptocurrencies.

3. **Tax Efficiency in Transfers**
Unlike traditional assets, Bitcoin can often be transferred across borders with minimal taxation. Consult with a financial advisor to navigate local regulations effectively.

Asset Growth Over Decades

Bitcoin's historical growth trajectory shows its potential as a long-term investment. Although it experiences short-term volatility, its overall trend has been upward. Holding Bitcoin for decades creates opportunities for compounding wealth.

Example of Generational Planning:

Anna sets up a family trust with $500,000 worth of Bitcoin.

- The trust uses Bitcoin as collateral for loans, generating $25,000 annually in passive income.
- Meanwhile, Bitcoin appreciates at an average annual rate of 10%.

- After 20 years, the trust holds over $3 million in Bitcoin and has generated $500,000 in passive income.

This combination of growth and income creates a self-sustaining engine for wealth transfer.

Advanced Estate Planning Strategies

To go a level deeper, consider how Bitcoin integrates with advanced financial tools:

1. **Multi-Signature Wallets for Security**
   Use multi-signature wallets to ensure that control over Bitcoin is shared among trusted family members or advisors. This prevents unauthorized access while enabling secure transfers.

2. **Life Insurance Policies Tied to Bitcoin**
   Some innovative financial products now allow you to fund life insurance with Bitcoin. This creates an additional layer of security for heirs while preserving the underlying asset.

3. **Dynamic Allocation in Trusts**
   A Bitcoin-focused trust can allocate funds dynamically, reinvesting profits into additional Bitcoin during market dips or using gains to

diversify into other asset classes.

Legacy Planning with Bitcoin

Legacy planning is about more than wealth; it's about providing future generations with the tools and mindset to succeed. Bitcoin is an ideal asset for this purpose because it aligns with the evolving financial landscape:

- It promotes financial independence.
- It's adaptable to a decentralized global economy.
- It offers flexibility in how wealth is stored and transferred.

Navigating Cross-Border Wealth Transfer

One of Bitcoin's standout advantages is its borderless nature. Unlike traditional assets that are subject to complex international tax laws, Bitcoin can be transferred seamlessly across borders.

Key Benefits:

- Avoid heavy taxation during international transfers.

- Provide heirs in different countries with equal access to wealth.
- Maintain control of assets regardless of geopolitical changes.

Example: David's International Legacy

David, a business owner, wants to ensure his children, who live in different countries, have equal access to his wealth. He holds $2 million in Bitcoin and creates a multi-signature wallet with the following features:

1. Each child has a unique access key.
2. A family lawyer holds the final signature key for added security.

Upon David's passing, the Bitcoin is distributed seamlessly to his children without the delays, fees, or complications typical of international asset transfers.

The Role of Passive Income

Bitcoin's role in generational wealth isn't just about capital gains. By leveraging Bitcoin to generate passive income, families can create a sustainable system that supports multiple generations.

1. **Using Bitcoin-Backed Loans**
   Generate cash flow by borrowing against Bitcoin and investing in income-generating assets like real estate or dividend stocks.

2. **Staking for Additional Yields**
   Some cryptocurrencies, including Bitcoin derivatives, allow staking for yield. While riskier, this can be an option for increasing cash flow in a family trust.

Advanced Insight: Bitcoin as a Family Business

Incorporate Bitcoin into a broader financial strategy by treating it like a family business:

- Use Bitcoin profits to fund entrepreneurial ventures for younger generations.
- Reinvest family business profits into Bitcoin to grow the overall portfolio.
- Develop financial literacy programs within your family to ensure long-term success.

Final Thoughts

Bitcoin isn't just a tool for today; it's a bridge to the future. By integrating it into your generational wealth strategy, you create a financial legacy that adapts to changing economic conditions while preserving and growing wealth.

The key is to think holistically:

- Combine Bitcoin with other diversified assets.
- Educate heirs about managing decentralized wealth.
- Leverage Bitcoin's unique advantages to outpace traditional wealth-building methods.

With careful planning, Bitcoin can become the cornerstone of a legacy that empowers your family for generations to come.

The Future of Bitcoin in a Decentralized Economy

As the world marches toward decentralization, Bitcoin stands as a cornerstone of this evolving financial paradigm. It's more than just a digital asset; Bitcoin is a transformational force reshaping how we think about money, trade, wealth building, and legacy. While many cryptocurrencies have emerged, none hold the timeless quality, security, and purpose-driven design that Bitcoin offers. It is the evolution of money—a financial revolution with profound implications for personal finance, global economics, and the transfer of generational wealth.

Bitcoin: An Evolution of Money

Money has always been a tool for facilitating trade, building wealth, and transferring value across generations. From bartering to gold, fiat currency, and now Bitcoin, each iteration of money has brought improvements in efficiency, security, and scalability.

Bitcoin elevates this progression:

- **Scarcity:** Unlike fiat currencies, which can be printed indefinitely, Bitcoin's capped supply ensures it retains value over time, mimicking and even surpassing gold's scarcity.

- **Trustless System:** With Bitcoin, trust shifts from institutions to immutable code and cryptographic principles, eliminating the need for central authorities.
- **Global Accessibility:** Bitcoin operates 24/7, transcending borders and making financial inclusion possible for billions who are excluded from traditional banking.

- **Timeless Utility:** While technologies come and go, Bitcoin's design ensures it remains relevant. Its decentralized ledger, consensus mechanisms, and growing adoption solidify its position as a timeless store of value.

Why Bitcoin Stands Apart from Other Cryptocurrencies

While thousands of cryptocurrencies have been created, Bitcoin remains unparalleled. It's not just a "first-mover advantage"—it's a matter of design, purpose, and execution.

1. **Immutable and Decentralized**
   Bitcoin's blockchain is the most secure and decentralized network in existence. Unlike other cryptocurrencies, which often compromise decentralization for speed or functionality,

Bitcoin's architecture prioritizes security and trustworthiness.

2. **Proven Track Record**
Bitcoin has survived over a decade of market cycles, technological challenges, and regulatory scrutiny. Many alternative cryptocurrencies have come and gone, but Bitcoin has consistently demonstrated resilience.

3. **Universal Adoption**
No other cryptocurrency has achieved Bitcoin's level of recognition, adoption, and integration into global financial systems. Central banks, institutional investors, and even nation-states (e.g., El Salvador) are now adopting Bitcoin as a reserve asset.

4. **Store of Value**
Unlike other cryptocurrencies that serve niche purposes or speculative trading, Bitcoin is widely regarded as "digital gold." Its primary role as a store of value makes it uniquely positioned to outlast fads and trends in the cryptocurrency space.

Bitcoin as a Timeless Trading Mechanism

From its inception, Bitcoin has redefined the mechanics of trade:

- **Borderless Transactions:** Trade happens without intermediaries or geographical restrictions, enabling seamless commerce between individuals and businesses worldwide.
- **Trustless Payments:** Bitcoin eliminates the risk of fraud and chargebacks, as every transaction is verified on the blockchain.
- **Instant Settlement:** Unlike traditional banking, which can take days to clear international transactions, Bitcoin provides near-instant settlement, revolutionizing trade logistics.
-

Bitcoin for Wealth Building

Bitcoin is more than a speculative asset; it is a foundational tool for building and compounding wealth in the modern age.

1. **Appreciation and Scarcity**
   With a fixed supply of 21 million coins, Bitcoin's value is inherently deflationary. As adoption grows, the supply-demand imbalance ensures that early holders are rewarded with exponential appreciation.

2. **Leveraging Bitcoin**
   Use Bitcoin as collateral to access loans for investments in other appreciating or income-generating assets, such as real estate or stocks.

3. **Diversification Through Bitcoin**
   Bitcoin's uncorrelated nature makes it an ideal hedge against traditional financial markets. It provides portfolio diversification, reducing overall risk.

4. **Passive Income Opportunities**
   Participate in decentralized finance (DeFi) platforms, earning yield through staking, lending, or providing liquidity using Bitcoin.

Bitcoin for Generational Wealth Transfer

Bitcoin is uniquely positioned to preserve and transfer wealth across generations:

- **Inflation Resistance:** Unlike fiat currencies, Bitcoin's value cannot be eroded by inflation, ensuring that wealth retains its purchasing power over decades.

- **Seamless Inheritance:** Digital wallets allow for direct and secure transfer to heirs without the complications of probate or excessive taxation.

- **Educational Opportunities:** By teaching heirs about Bitcoin and blockchain, families can instill financial literacy and adaptability in a rapidly changing world.

Example: Reina, a retired teacher, establishes a trust that holds $1 million in Bitcoin. Her heirs inherit not only the Bitcoin but also access to a family manual explaining Bitcoin's management and use. This ensures the wealth she passes down is preserved and grows under their stewardship.

Emerging Trends for Bitcoin in a Decentralized Economy

1. **Decentralized Finance (DeFi)**
   Bitcoin holders can use their assets to access DeFi platforms, earning yield through lending or liquidity provision. While Ethereum dominates this space, Bitcoin's entry into DeFi through Layer 2 solutions like the Lightning Network is expanding its utility.

2. **Global Adoption**
    - Nations adopting Bitcoin as legal tender or a reserve asset signal its growing legitimacy.
    - Institutions are integrating Bitcoin into traditional financial products like ETFs, increasing accessibility.

3. **Tokenization of Assets**
   Bitcoin can serve as the foundation for tokenizing real-world assets, such as real estate or art. This enables fractional ownership and liquidity for traditionally illiquid investments.

Positioning Yourself for the Future with Bitcoin

1. **Stay Informed**
   Continuously educate yourself about Bitcoin and blockchain developments. The technology is evolving rapidly, and staying ahead ensures you capitalize on new opportunities.

2. **Strategic Investments**
   Use Bitcoin-backed liquidity to participate in emerging markets, such as artificial intelligence, renewable energy, or decentralized applications.

3. **Sustainable Practices**
   Align Bitcoin investments with trends that prioritize sustainability, such as renewable energy-powered mining or projects focused on carbon offsets.

Example: Ethan's Strategy for the Decentralized Economy

Ethan borrows against his $500,000 Bitcoin portfolio to invest in a tokenized real estate project. The project yields annual returns of 8%, which he uses to pay down his loan. Meanwhile, his Bitcoin appreciates at an average rate of 10% per year. Over 15 years, Ethan's diversified investments provide financial security and exponential growth.

Why Bitcoin Is the Cornerstone of a Decentralized Future

Bitcoin's attributes make it uniquely suited to thrive in a decentralized economy:

- **Global Neutrality:** No nation controls Bitcoin, making it the ultimate global currency.

- **Censorship Resistance:** Bitcoin empowers individuals to transact freely without fear of interference.

- **Technological Evolution:** As the blockchain ecosystem matures, Bitcoin's use cases continue to expand, ensuring its relevance.

Final Thoughts

Bitcoin isn't just an asset—it's a movement. It represents freedom, innovation, and the democratization of finance. By embracing Bitcoin, you're not just participating in a financial revolution; you're positioning yourself, your family, and future generations to thrive in a decentralized world.

As the future unfolds, Bitcoin will continue to evolve, proving its timelessness as a mechanism for trade, wealth building, and generational prosperity. The question isn't whether Bitcoin will shape the future; it's whether you'll be ready to harness its potential.